Teaching and Learning With Bulletin Boards

A year's worth of interactive projects that can be incorporated into sensational bulletin boards!

Written for teachers by teachers
(who understand time and ideas and how scarce they are . . .)

Authors: Stacy M. Berg & Jean M. Sweeney

Illustrator: Carol Tiernon

Cover Design: Signature Design Group, Inc.

Project Manager: Mina McMullin
Production and Design: Jill Kaufman, Jennifer Sottoriva
Editor: Kathy Zaun

GOOD APPLE
A Division of Frank Schaffer Publications, Inc.
23740 Hawthorne Blvd.
Torrance, CA 90505

ISBN 1-56417-999-0

TABLE OF CONTENTS

* Beginning-of-the-year boards

∆ Seasonal boards

• Year-round boards

INTRODUCTION

*T*eaching and Learning With Bulletin Boards is the perfect tool for you to use to turn bulletin boards into exciting, hands-on learning projects for students! Packed with a year's worth of ideas and activities, you will love seeing your students motivated to participate in bulletin board projects that help them learn about topics in math, science, reading, language, art, music, etc., and about building self-esteem, self-awareness, and critical thinking skills.

A wonderful variety of patterns, parent letters, charts, and other forms accompany each project and provide a simple means for you to involve your students in these challenging, interactive activities. Also included for each are lesson objectives, easy-to-follow directions, and materials needed. You can choose from boards that display final projects or those that involve ongoing, incentive-based activities.

Most of the bulletin board projects featured can be used at any time during the year, although some are particularly suited to seasons and holidays. *Teaching and Learning With Bulletin Boards* is the perfect way for you to enjoy teaching while your students engage in fun-filled, challenging, educational activities!

AFTER MATH . . .

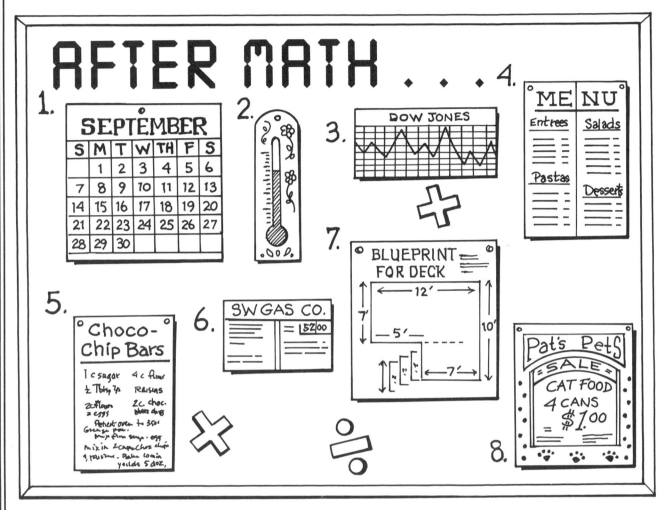

PURPOSE: To help students develop an awareness of the daily role math plays in the real world; To help students strengthen the relationship between math and real-life application

MATERIALS: a variety of these items brought in by students: advertisements, menus, utility bills, checks, blueprints, recipes, sports statistics, tape measures, thermometers, calendars; one copy of activity pages 6 and 7 per student

DIRECTIONS: Discuss with students how math is all around us. Brainstorm how math is used in everyday life. Ask students to bring in two samples of real-world math from the list above. On activity page 6, have students write as many math concepts as they can find on each sample. Collect samples and activity pages from students. Hang the samples on the board, numbering each. Choose two samples daily and have students fill out activity page 7. Go over activity page 7 for each sample item. See how many different math concepts were identified for each sample.

After Math

Name _____

Item # _____

My example of real life math is _____.

This example uses the following math concepts:

1. _____
2. _____
3. _____
4. _____
5. _____

- -

After Math

Name _____

Item # _____

My example of real life math is _____.

This example uses the following math concepts:

1. _____
2. _____
3. _____
4. _____
5. _____

After Math

Name _____

Item # _____

I have identified the following math concepts:

1. _____

2. _____

3. _____

4. _____

5. _____

- -

After Math

Name _____

Item # _____

I have identified the following math concepts:

1. _____

2. _____

3. _____

4. _____

5. _____

PURPOSE: To help students practice creative writing skills by sharing objects that are special to them

MATERIALS: one copy of activity pages 9 and 10 per student; copies of page 11, enlarged or reduced, to be used as art on the bulletin board

DIRECTIONS: Explain to students that their families (including pets) have volunteered to go to another planet for an extended period of time. Give each student a copy of the invitation on page 9. Have students fold it on the dotted lines and fill out the information asked for. Tell students that they may each take one item with them that has significant value to them. This object cannot be one that can be replaced on the planet (toys, games, etc.). Have students bring in their objects and discuss them with their classmates. They can then turn this shared experience into a writing assignment using page 10, which will be displayed on the bulletin board. Students can write about the planet they will be visiting or about the experience they had there. Brainstorm possibilities as a class. For more alien fun, take a picture of each child and his or her object and display these next to students' papers.

To an Alien Vacation . . .

Yes, it's true! Aliens have landed and have come for a visit! But don't be upset. They would like you and your family to join them on their planet. There, you will study the lifestyles of these strange beings, and they will learn more about you!

Fortunately, all of the conveniences of "home" will be provided. (They are extremely advanced—computer games, TVs, VCRs, etc., are all part of their culture!) However, you must bring the most valuable item you own so as not to forget your fellow earthlings and the memories you cherish.

List on the back of this invitation the top five items you would consider taking. Then put a star next to the one object you choose to take.

IRREPLACEABLE ITEMS

1. _____

2. _____

3. _____

4. _____

5. _____

YOU'RE INVITED . . .

9

Alien Vacation

Blabber Mouth

PURPOSE: To creatively display students' writing (This board is particularly well-suited for expository or persuasive pieces.)

MATERIALS: one copy of the Blabber Mouth on pages 13 and 14 per student, tape, markers, colored pencils, one finished writing piece per student

DIRECTIONS: Upon completion of the final edit of students' writing pieces, have students assemble the Blabber Mouth by taping the two pages together. Have students color and write their final copy onto their Blabber Mouths. Display them on the bulletin board.

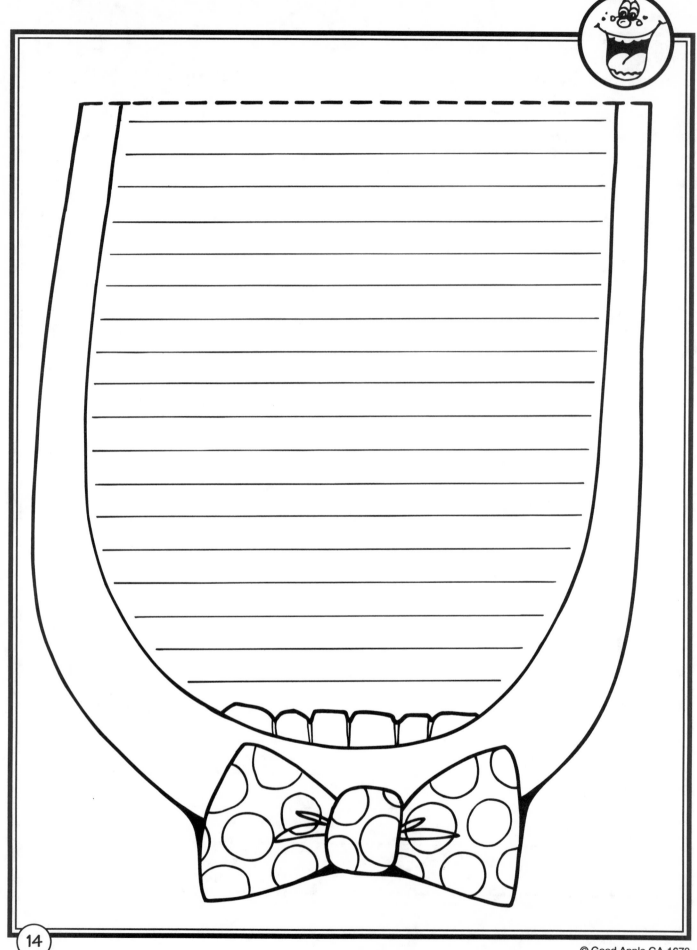

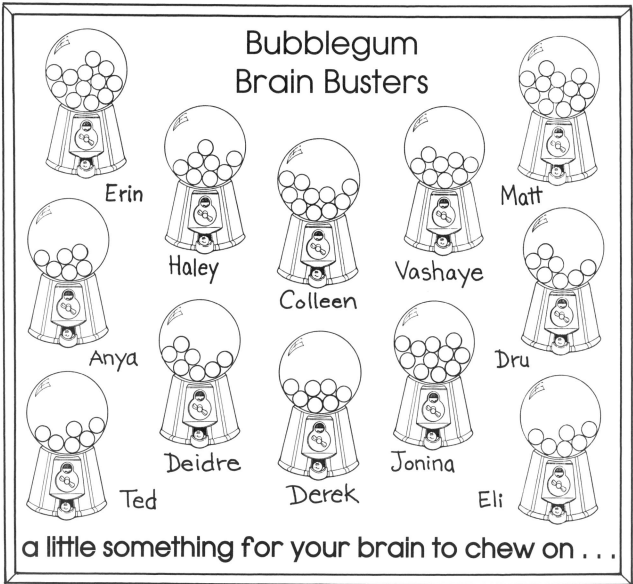

Bubblegum Brain Busters

Erin

Haley

Colleen

Vashaye

Matt

Anya

Deidre

Dru

Ted

Derek

Jonina

Eli

a little something for your brain to chew on . . .

PURPOSE: To have students use problem-solving skills to examine and respond to brain teaser-type questions

MATERIALS: one copy of the gumball machine on pages 18 and 19 per student, gumballs made from construction paper or gumball stickers, trivia questions (Sample questions are provided on pages 16 and 17.)

DIRECTIONS: Put up a Bubblegum Brain Buster (trivia question) of the day on the board or overhead. Each time a student correctly responds to a question, give him or her a gumball for his or her machine. After a particular number of gumballs are earned (teacher discretion), give the student a pack of bubblegum or some other reward.

Bubblegum Brain Busters

Q: If today is Wednesday, is the day that follows the day that comes after the day that precedes the day before yesterday Tuesday?

A: yes

Q: Change 1, 2, and 3 to three different letters of the alphabet so that each of these numbers will become a word: 123, 312, 231.

A: tea, ate, eat

Q: What 6-letter word has four *u*'s in it?

A: muumuu

Q: What letter of the alphabet is used more than 50 times in the name of the 50 states?

A: the letter **a**

Q: Rearrange the letters in "O, Wonder" to make one word.

A: one word

Q: What three words in the English language end with *gry*?

A: hungry, angry, pugry (a turban)

Q: Think of a number. Double it. Add 10. Divide by 2. Subtract the original number. What is ALWAYS the result?

A: 5

Q: Form an English word from these letters: p s s s s s e e e e l l n.

A: sleeplessness

Q: Which state in the United States of America has a name that is round at both ends and high in the center?

A: Ohio

Q: What is an eight-letter word that contains only one vowel?

A: strength

Q: If six coins total 48¢, the six coins will consist of how many quarters, dimes, nickels, and pennies?

A: 1 quarter, 2 dimes, 0 nickels, and 3 pennies

Q: If v = vowel and c = consonant, can you find words with vcvcvcvc and cvcvcvcv patterns?

A: enamored and parasite

Q: Think of a number. Multiply it by 2. Add 18 to the product. Divide by 2. Subtract the original number. What is the result?

A: 9

Q: What 11-letter word has five *a*'s but no other vowels in it?

A: abracadabra

Bubblegum Brain Busters

I slept	✓ YEARLY	Hi Ho Ag
A: I overslept.	A: yearly check-up	A: hi, ho, silver

t o w n	wear long	o u t
A: downtown	A: long underwear	A: outside

TUNE TUNE TUNE TUNE	EMOCLEW
A: fortune	A: welcome back

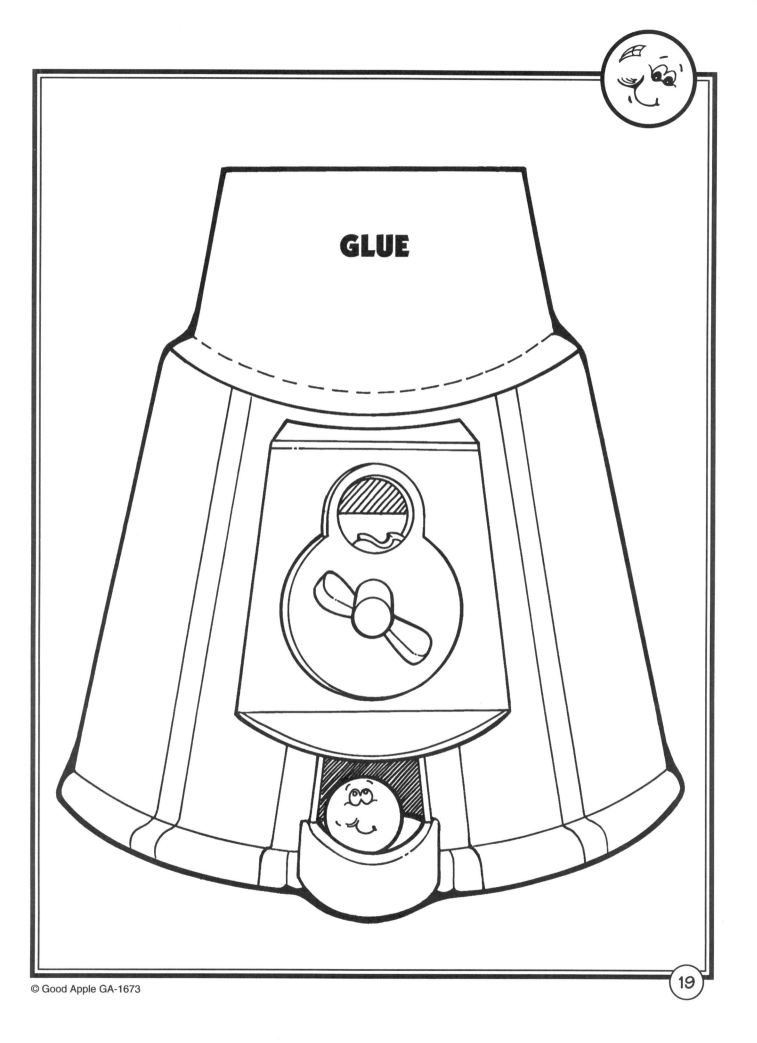

GLUE

COVER STORY

PURPOSE: To have students create book covers for chosen novels

MATERIALS: one copy of page 21 per student, a variety of book covers, large sheets of construction paper, crayons, markers, colored pencils, etc. (Magazine cutouts can also be used in addition to students' original artwork.)

DIRECTIONS: Discuss with students what draws a reader to choose a particular book. Further discuss the importance of the cover design in relation to the success of the book. Explain that many people tend to choose books based on their appearance. Have each student design a cover for a novel of his or her choice after having read it. Display them all over the board.

NOTE: You could also have students write book summaries to be displayed on the book flaps.

DEAR AUTHOR

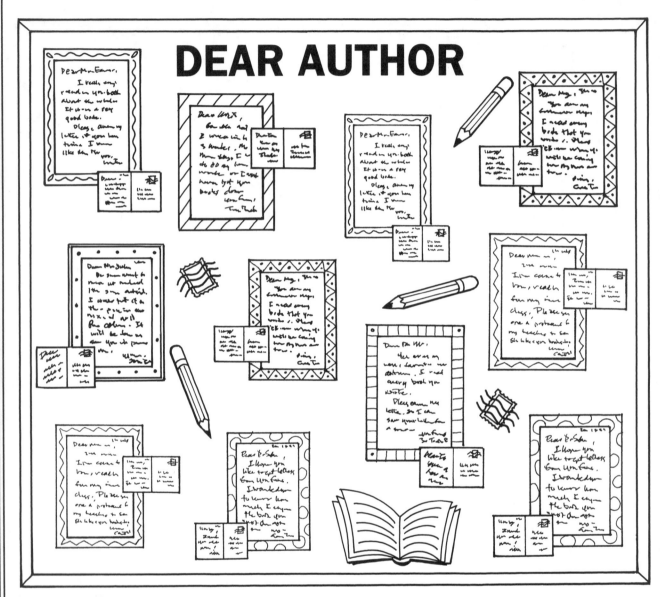

PURPOSE: To help students establish a link between reader and author

MATERIALS: self-addressed, stamped postcards; a variety of stationery and envelopes

DIRECTIONS: After reading a novel of his or her choice, have each student write to the author discussing favorite events, characters, or writing techniques and include a self-addressed postcard. Students can request that the authors return the postcards with a personal note. Copy students' original letters and display them on the board. As postcards are returned, place them next to the students' letters.

NOTE: Prior to students writing letters, brainstorm with them ideas for writing letters and discuss letter format. Postcards can be purchased from the post office.

Every Cloud Has a Silver Lining

PURPOSE: To have students evaluate a situation and recognize that one can look positively upon almost any event

MATERIALS: one copy of the cloud pattern on page 24 per student, silver glitter, glue

DIRECTIONS: Discuss with students world events, problems in novels, and/or personal situations that, upon first look, may be unfortunate but actually have positive outcomes. Students may write about these events, including the positive outcomes, on their clouds and then outline them with silver glitter.

NOTE: Give students time to discuss and prewrite before finalizing their drafts for display purposes. Share the events as a class, and then have each student hang his or her personal cloud on the bulletin board.

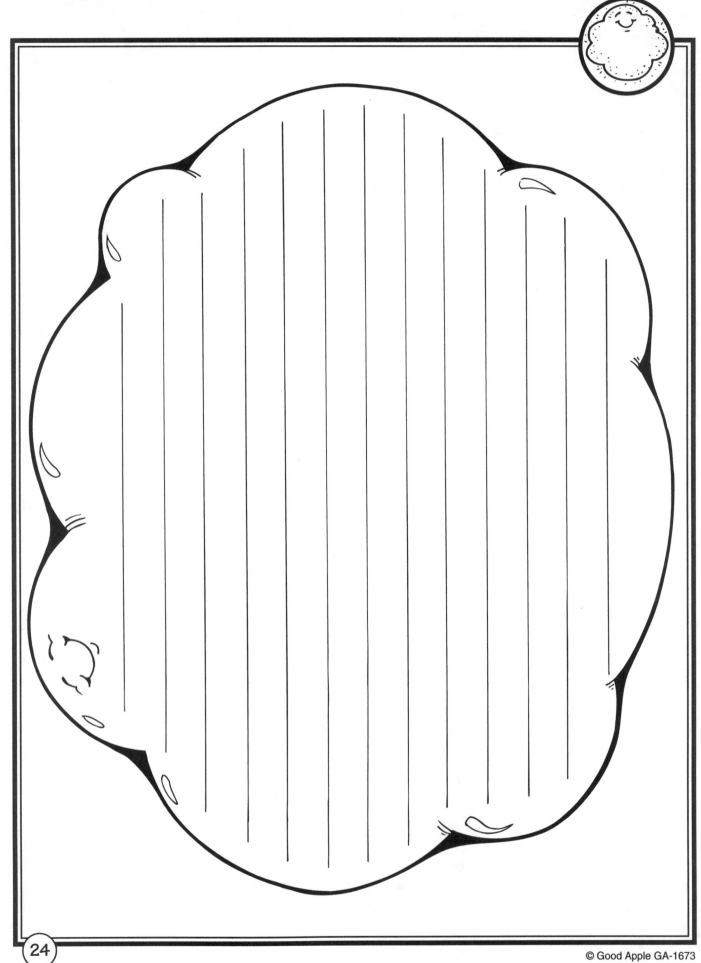

GIVE 'EM A HAND!

PURPOSE: To build a supportive classroom environment while encouraging students to look for the best in one another; To build self-esteem in all students

MATERIALS: copies of the patterns on page 26; slips of paper, each containing a student's name

DIRECTIONS: Discuss with students the importance of recognizing that everyone possesses special and unique qualities. Each day, draw the name of a student. This will be the featured student about whom each student will write a positive quality on one of the sign patterns. Each sign should depict an attribute that is unique to the featured student, focusing on the POSITIVE! Students may select from any one of the three patterns or draw their own.

NOTE: You may choose to do this in conjunction with the "SPOTLIGHT ON . . ." bulletin board (pages 75–76) allowing students to take home their signs when their time in the "spotlight" has come to an end.

APRIL GREAT EIGHT

PURPOSE: To provide a variety of independent activities from which students may choose three to complete for a particular month

MATERIALS: an activity list for each month of the school year (This list could be laminated and posted on the board with individual copies given to each student.), paper, magazines, crayons, markers, etc.

NOTE: Eight sample activities have been provided for September through June on pages 28–36. Use these with your students, if appropriate, or create activities more suited to your students' needs.

DIRECTIONS: Read and display the activities at the beginning of each month. Students are to choose three of the eight activities to complete by a prearranged deadline. Display the completed activities on the board.

September Great Eight

1. Write a letter to me describing yourself in detail.

2. Make up an acrostic for September. Use "September" words.

3. List the top ten qualities you believe a good teacher possesses.

4. Write a paper describing your favorite school memory.

5. Find three recipes which have apples in them. Write each one neatly on a card. Try to bake or cook using one of the recipes. Share the result with the class.

6. Write a paragraph describing your perfect day.

7. Create a back-to-school song or poem.

8. List and explain what you would buy for yourself if you had five dollars.

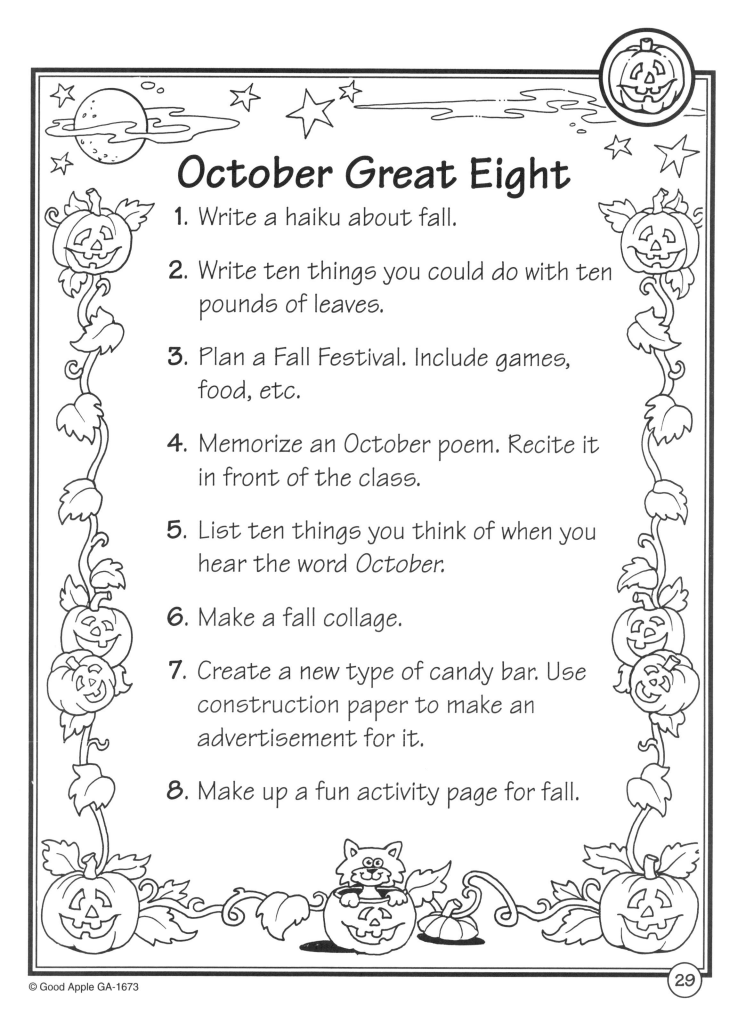

October Great Eight

1. Write a haiku about fall.

2. Write ten things you could do with ten pounds of leaves.

3. Plan a Fall Festival. Include games, food, etc.

4. Memorize an October poem. Recite it in front of the class.

5. List ten things you think of when you hear the word *October*.

6. Make a fall collage.

7. Create a new type of candy bar. Use construction paper to make an advertisement for it.

8. Make up a fun activity page for fall.

November Great Eight

1. Write things you are thankful for using each letter in the word THANKSGIVING.

2. Write a poem from a turkey's point of view on Thanksgiving.

3. Prepare a Thanksgiving feast. Write or draw what you would eat.

4. Name one thing that pops into your head about November. Explain.

5. Using the letters in the word THANKSGIVING, come up with as many new words as you can.

6. Make a November calendar. For each day, write something nice you will do for someone else.

7. Bring in an article related to Thanksgiving or autumn. Mount it on paper and discuss it with the class.

8. Make up a comic strip involving a turkey.

December Great Eight

1. Using magazine pictures, make a collage or greeting card celebrating winter.

2. Design a two-week itinerary for your winter break. Where will you go? What will you do?

3. Write and discuss ten places you'd take an out-of-town guest in your city or town.

4. Tell about ten things you'd do to brighten someone's day. Do five of these!

5. Design a winter decoration to hang in the classroom.

6. Find a positive article showing people helping others. Share it with the class.

7. Tell how you would spend $100 on your family. Be specific and cut out or draw your own pictures.

8. Create a mobile showing winter/holiday activities.

January Great Eight

1. Create a thank-you card, thanking someone for your favorite gift.

2. List ten things you would do if school was canceled due to bad weather.

3. List ten things you would take with you on vacation.

4. Write a paragraph describing how you spent New Year's Eve.

5. Draw a picture of how you feel today and another showing how you'd like to feel.

6. Bring in a picture of yourself from last year and one from this year. List ten ways you have changed.

7. Design a car of the future.

8. Tell some ways you would like to improve as a student and/or person for the new year.

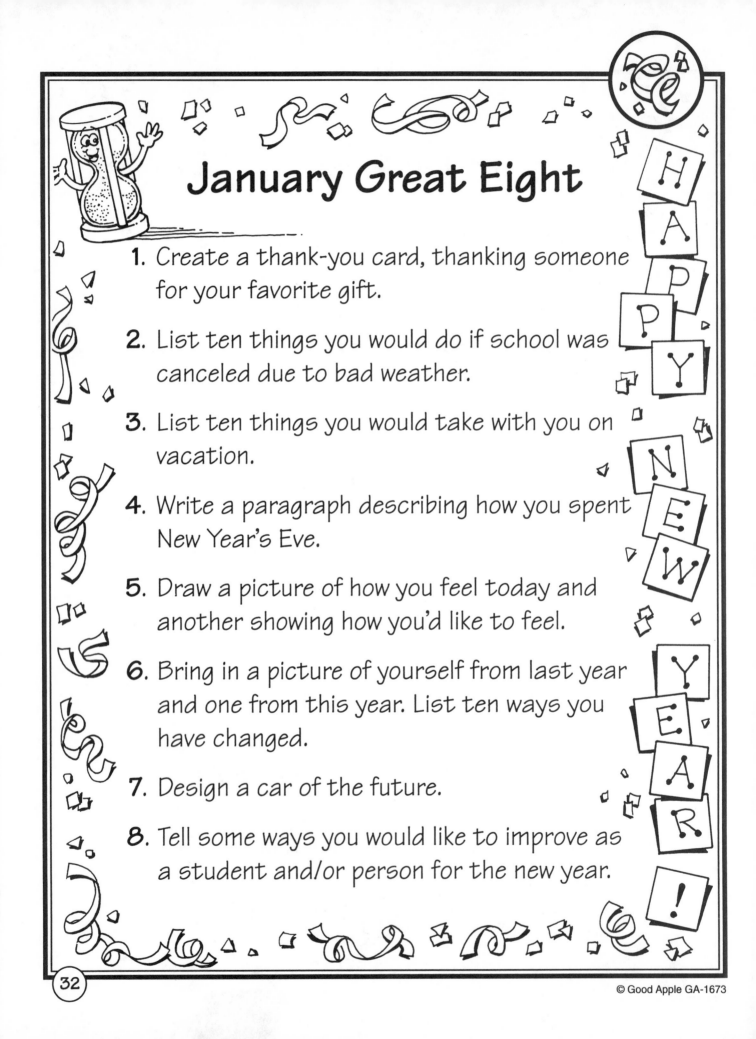

February Great Eight

1. Make an original Valentine's Day card. Use colored paper, magazine clippings, stickers, etc.

2. Write about one famous African American and describe his or her accomplishments.

3. Find and write about someone born on February 29th. (A Leap Year baby!)

4. Create a puzzle or word search for Presidents' Day.

5. Write two nouns, two verbs, and two adjectives for each letter in the word LOVE.

6. Research and report on the history of Valentine's Day.

7. Choose a love song and play it for the class. Describe how it makes you feel.

8. Write a letter to your parents telling them why you love them.

March Great Eight

1. Who is St. Patrick? Research and write a short summary about him.

2. Do you "March to the beat of a different drummer?" Why or why not? If so, how?

3. Write a limerick about March or St. Patrick's Day.

4. Discuss five items you consider lucky.

5. March "comes in like a lion and goes out like a lamb." List ten ways this can be proven.

6. Design an original kite.

7. Bring in ten green items and explain their importance.

8. Choose a holiday celebrated in March. Write a brief history of it.

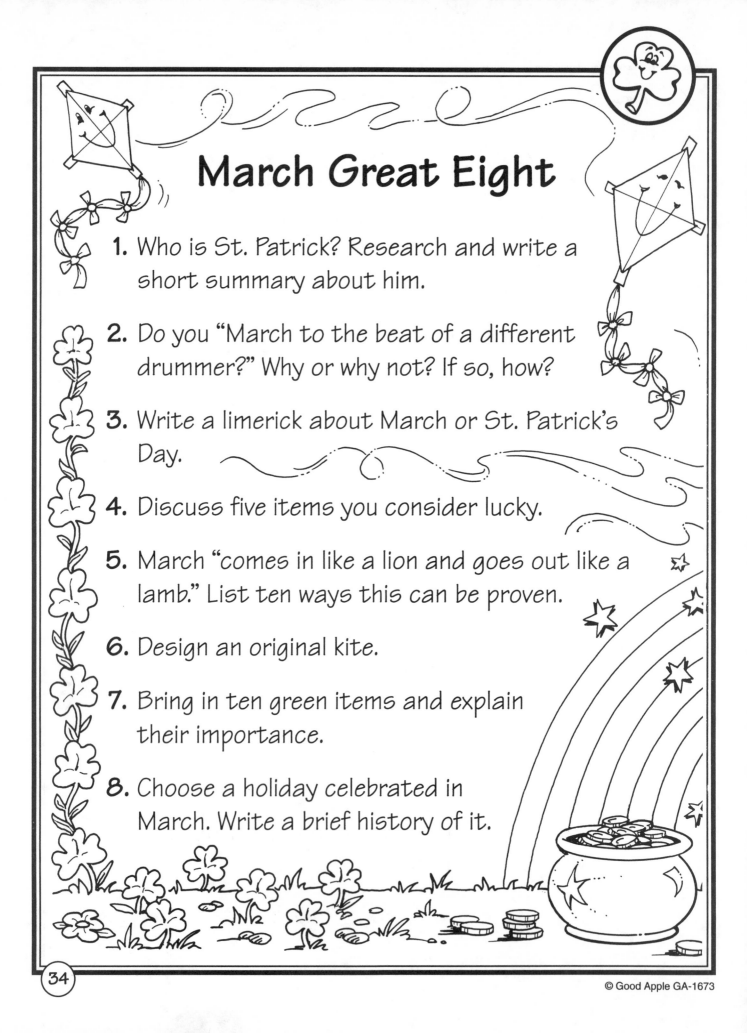

April Great Eight

1. Write a paragraph telling about the best April Fool's prank you ever played.

2. Tell what you would do on a rainy April day.

3. Design an original umbrella.

4. Write a one-page paper on a holiday celebrated in April.

5. Create a poster in celebration of Earth Day.

6. Find out when International Children's Book Day is and bring in your favorite book. Discuss it in class.

7. Color the first initial of your name. Use spring colors!

8. In a story format, write about the life of a raindrop from its point of view.

May/June Great Eight

1. If April showers bring May flowers, what do May flowers bring?

2. List 5–7 books you plan to read this summer. What made you select these?

3. In one paragraph, explain the tradition of May Day.

4. List ten things you plan to do this summer.

5. Choose one vacation spot and write an itinerary of your planned trip.

6. Write an acrostic for the phrase "Summer Vacation."

7. Draw or create colorful cards for Mother's Day and Father's Day.

8. List ten things you've enjoyed most about this school year.

THE GREAT GRAFFITI BOARD

PURPOSE: To encourage students to express themselves through informal drawings and written expression; To encourage students to work together and respect others' work while incorporating their own work into an existing piece

MATERIALS: light-colored butcher paper, copies of the brick pattern on page 38, markers

DIRECTIONS: After hanging the butcher paper, place bricks on the board to represent a wall. Have students write messages, draw pictures, etc., on the wall. The title can be written in marker, or cut-out letters can be used.

NOTE: An alternative idea is to trace the bricks onto a piece of butcher paper, then have students draw on them. After the graffiti board has been taken down, it can be cut into large puzzle-shaped pieces, laminated, and used as a floor puzzle.

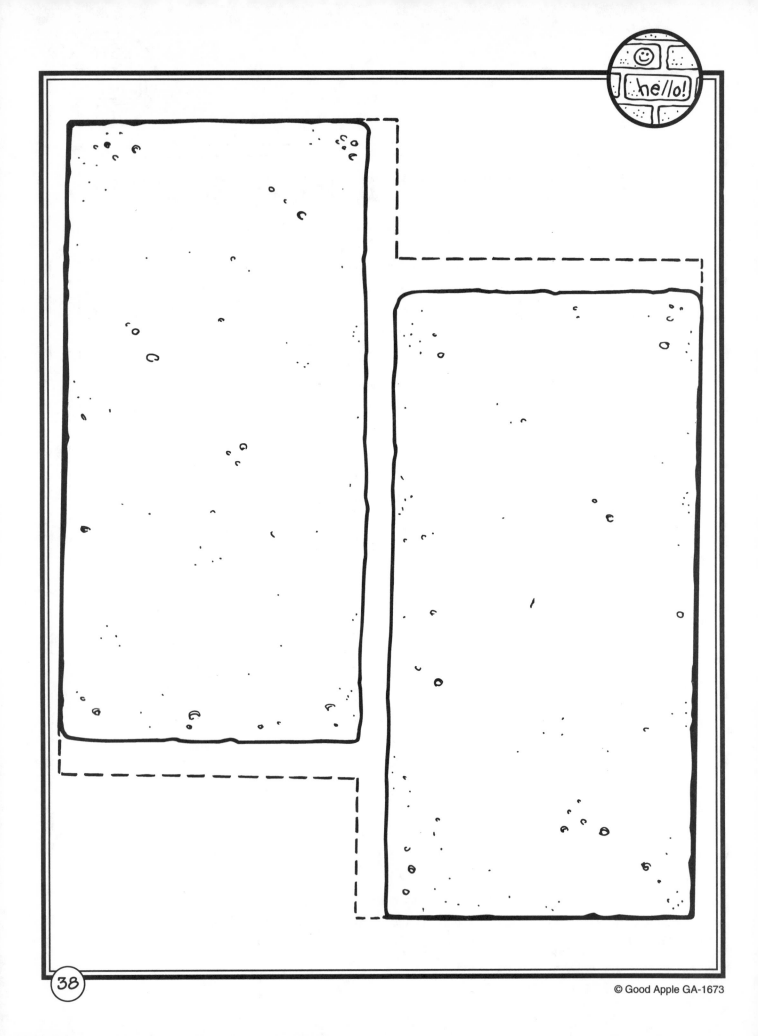

PURPOSE: To begin the school year helping students set social and academic goals

MATERIALS: Happy New Year horns, noisemakers, streamers, one copy of the resolution sheet on page 40 per student (Make photocopies using a variety of colors if possible.)

DIRECTIONS: Give students copies of page 40. On them, have students write goals (resolutions) relating to the beginning of a new school year. Have students sign and date them, and display them on the board.

NOTE: Prior to students finalizing their resolutions, discuss the importance of goal-setting and the meaning of the word *resolution*. This is an excellent board to use for display during open house. Resolution sheets can be saved for portfolios or conferences.

My New Year's Resolutions

HOW SWEET IT IS!

PURPOSE: To help students start the school year in a "sweet" way

MATERIALS: one colored bag per student; copies of page 42; a variety of candy, treats, stickers, etc.

DIRECTIONS: Cut apart the strips on page 42. Personalize each colored bag with a student's name and attach it to the board using thumbtacks. Reward good behavior, a job well done, etc., with a sweet strip. Students store the strips in their treat bags as they are earned. At the end of a designated time period, students can trade in sweet strips for candy. (Candy, sugarless gum, cookies, stickers, etc., may be given.)

NOTE: This may also be done during October or February, taking the board down and distributing treats during a Fall Festival or on Valentine's Day. Treat bags can be obtained often at no cost from candy stores. Another low-cost alternative would be to have students decorate brown or white lunch bags.

I AM SO PROUD!

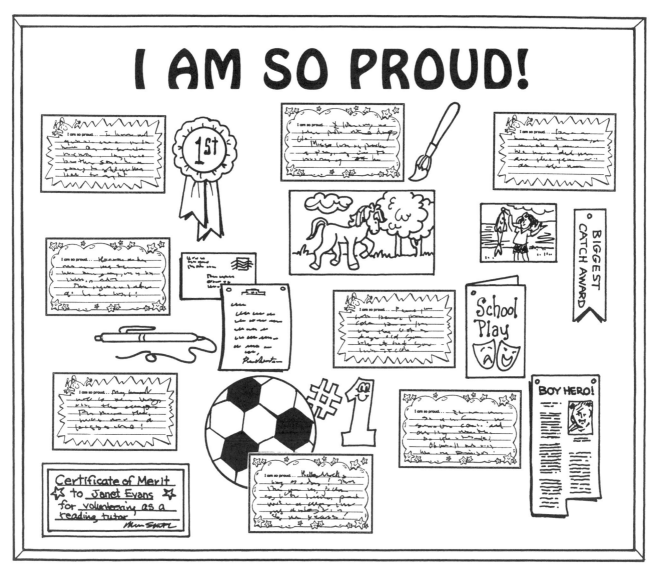

PURPOSE: To help students share, through writing, an academic, social, or personal accomplishment

MATERIALS: colored copies of page 44

DIRECTIONS: Give each student half of page 44. Explain to students that they will be sharing an accomplishment that was important to them. This must be something they've worked toward, not a material possession. However, they will be bringing in an object which is associated with their accomplishment (photos, ribbons, newspaper articles, etc.).

NOTE: Give students time to discuss and prewrite before finalizing their drafts for display purposes. Share them as a class and display objects brought in by students.

I am so proud . . . _____

_____

_____

_____

_____

_____

I am so proud . . . _____

_____

_____

_____

_____

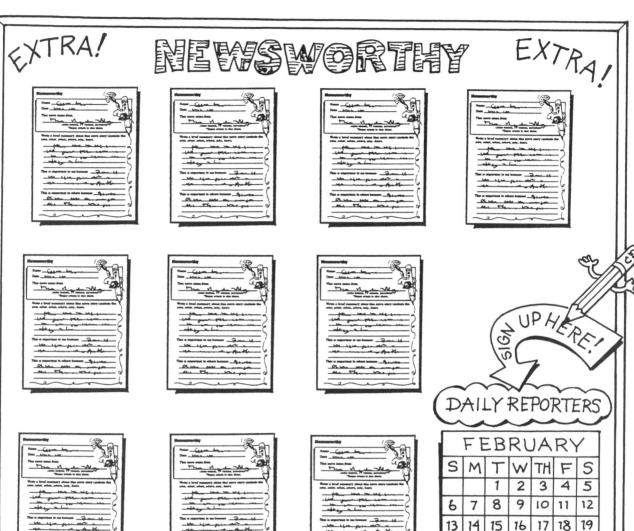

PURPOSE: To display current events, school newsletters, menus, calendars, etc.

MATERIALS: precut letters spelling *Newsworthy* from newspapers, a large calendar, one copy of page 46 per student

DIRECTIONS: Assign each student one day per month on which he or she will report a current event from radio, television, news magazines, or newspapers. Give students copies of page 46 and have them follow this format. Allow time for students to share their events and then display their pages on the board.

NOTE: You may want to suggest to students to bring in positive stories. As well, you may want to limit the number and type of sports events.

Newsworthy

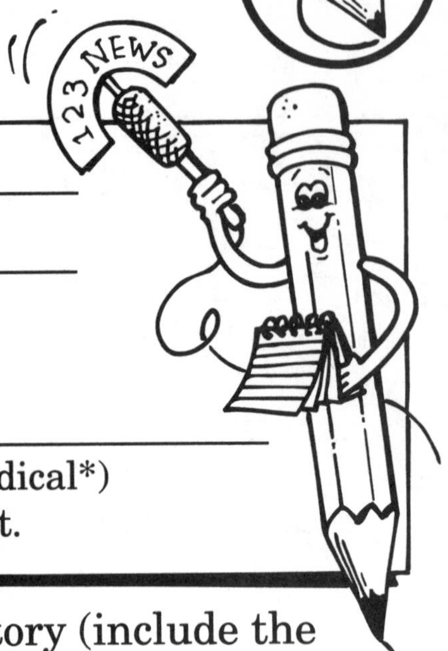

Name _____

Date _____

This news came from

_____

(radio station, TV station, periodical*)
*Staple article to this sheet.

Write a brief summary about this news story (include the *who, what, when, where, why, how*).

_____

_____

_____

_____

_____

This is important to me because _____

_____

_____

_____

This is important to others because _____

_____

_____

_____

PERFECTLY PREPARED POETRY PICNIC

PURPOSE: To have students creatively display original poetry

MATERIALS: construction paper and crayons/markers (for students to use to create their picnic items); red and white paper (for students to use to create picnic tablecloths, or a purchased plastic or paper tablecloth will work for students to use); one copy of the invitation on page 48 per student; one copy of the list of foods on page 49 per student which students are expected to "bring"; copies of the ant patterns (page 50)

DIRECTIONS: Attach the tablecloth (made or bought) to the board as a background. Give each student an invitation. Have students fold it. Next, have each student select a different item from the menu on page 49. (You could also assign items on students' invitations if you prefer.) Students will create their items using construction paper, incorporating poems they write into their designs. Students' poems should be about their delicious picnic items.

NOTE: Invitations to the "picnic" can be mailed home if you choose to do so. An actual picnic lunch can be held in the classroom at which time students can share their picnic items and poems and attach them to the picnic board. The following day, you can scatter ants all over the board.

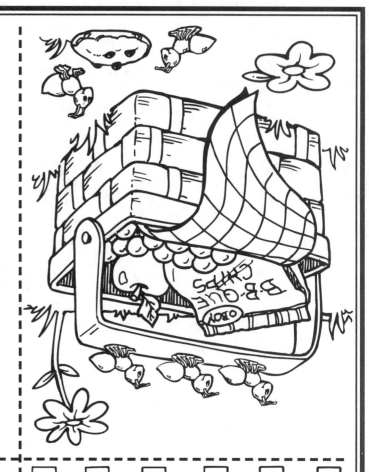

You're Invited to a Picnic!

It's a picnic, that is true!
Something fun for me and you!
You're to bring something
to eat . . .
A delicious picnic treat!
BUT . . . instead of eating it,
you are to WRITE
a poem that is out of sight!
There will be paper on which you can design.
Just remember, it need not rhyme!
Your item is

_____.

48

Perfectly Prepared Picnic Items

corn on the cob

baked beans

watermelon

hamburgers

hot dogs

lemonade

chocolate chip
cookies

coleslaw

Jell–O

grapes

deviled eggs

ice cream

ketchup

mustard

pickles

brownies

s'mores

fried chicken

potato salad

strawberries

cherries

sandwiches

potato chips

fruit salad

carrot cake

pretzels

juice

soda

PICTURE PERFECT

Say Cheese!

snap!

Snap!

snap!

Smile!

snap!

PURPOSE: To get acquainted with your new class; This is an excellent first-day-of-school activity which can then be displayed at open house.

MATERIALS: one copy page of 52 per student, a photo of each student (Optional: colored pencils for students to use to fill out page 52.) Note: Photos can be brought from home or taken at school.

DIRECTIONS: Have students complete page 52 and then spend time sharing their pages with a partner and/or with the class. If students do paired sharing, they can then introduce their partners to the class. Collect and display students' pages with their photos on a bulletin board.

Picture Perfect

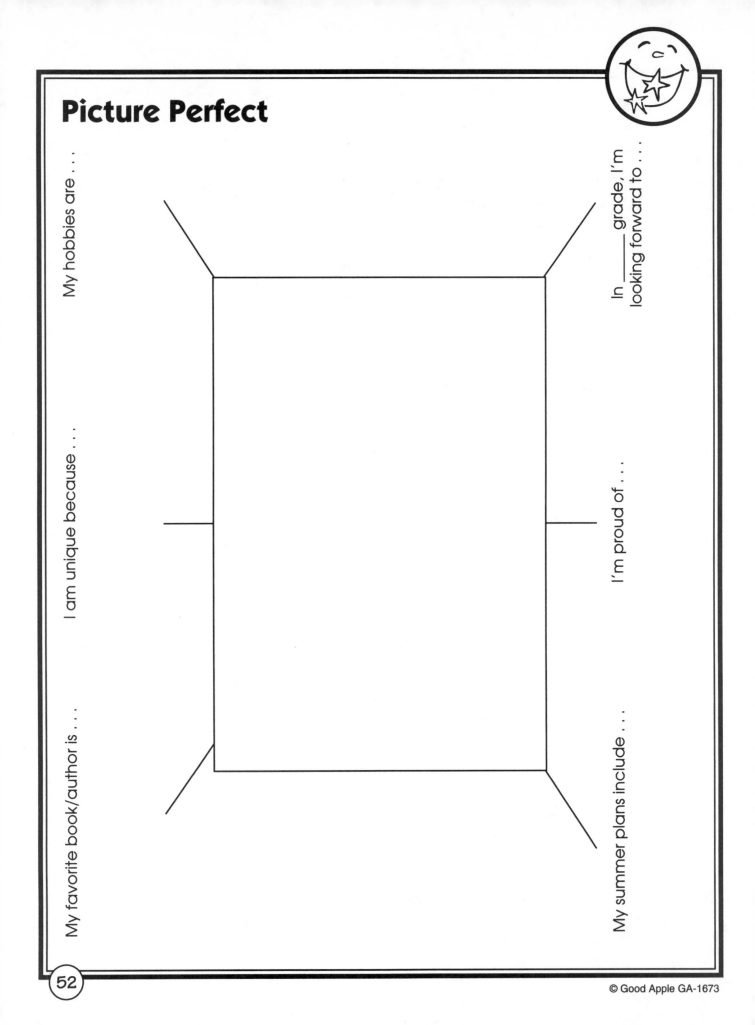

My hobbies are . . .

In _____ grade, I'm looking forward to . . . .

I am unique because . . . .

I'm proud of . . . .

My favorite book/author is . . . .

My summer plans include . . . .

HISTORICAL POSTCARDS FROM THE EDGE

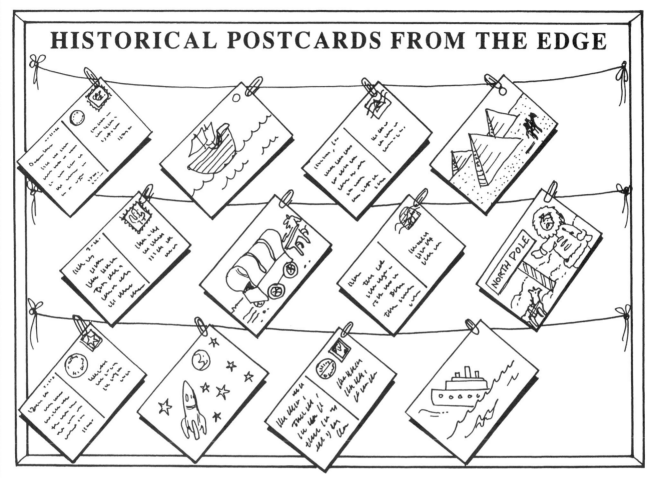

PURPOSE: To have students create postcards that incorporate factual knowledge about historical people or events; Students' work should reflect an understanding of the time period involved.

MATERIALS: tagboard or heavy construction paper for final draft, string or yarn for hanging, paper clips, copies of sample postcards (page 54)

DIRECTIONS: Have students select historical figures or events to research. Students will need to know where their event was located or where the person was from, the year in which the event took place, and the location to which the postcard is to be sent. One side of the postcard should feature the illustration, while the other should contain the letter and address information. Be sure to discuss illustrations, postmarks, language, and information relevant to the time period. Also make sure students understand that they need to include factual information in their letters as well. (See sample postcards on page 54.)

NOTE: Postcards can be laminated or covered with clear contact paper to give them a finished look. Hang string on the bulletin board and use paper clips to display postcards.

Historical Postcards From the Edge

Dear Miguel,

    Will you travel with me on my voyage? I kidnapped 57 Indians, and we can sell them as slaves. Meet me in the northern part of the New World. The shortest way is across the Atlantic Ocean. On your way, stop in Greenland. When I visited it, I thought I discovered a new land, but it looked as though someone had already been there. We should be back in three years. With your help, I hope we will discover gold and spices.

              Love,

              Gaspar

Miguel Corte-real
153 Itaska Blvd.
Lisbon, Portugal
      15LP32A

Dear Felipa, my beloved wife,

    I am at sea right now. I am missing you more than I can say. Even though I've only been gone since August of 1492, it seems like much longer. How are you and Diego? I am traveling on the Atlantic Ocean. I plan on returning in a couple of months. Oh my! Someone on the crew saw land. I have to go now. I'm going to be famous!

    Love & kisses,

    Christopher Columbus

Mrs. Christopher Columbus
1451 Genoa Dr.
Porta Santo, Spain 15060

Problem of the Day

TODAY'S PROBLEM

Using a 3x3 square, arrange the odd numbers (1-17) so that they total 27 in all directions.

PURPOSE: To present a daily problem-solving situation that students solve independently

MATERIALS: copies of the pea pod and pea patterns on page 56, a variety of problem-solving situations (See samples on pages 57 and 58.)

DIRECTIONS: Create a pea pod and peas using the patterns. Enlarge the patterns to fit your board. Display them on the bulletin board. Display one problem each day on a single pea. Provide a five- or ten-minute opportunity for students to read and begin solving the "Problem of the Day." (Sample problems are provided on pages 57 and 58. Feel free to use these or others you design that better meet the needs of your class.) Responses can be written in pea pod journals created by students which you can collect weekly if you choose. Answers may be discussed daily or collected at the end of the week.

NOTE: This board can be used for any curricular area, but is especially suited for math. You may want to have printed copies of the "Problem of the Day" available for students who need written guides.

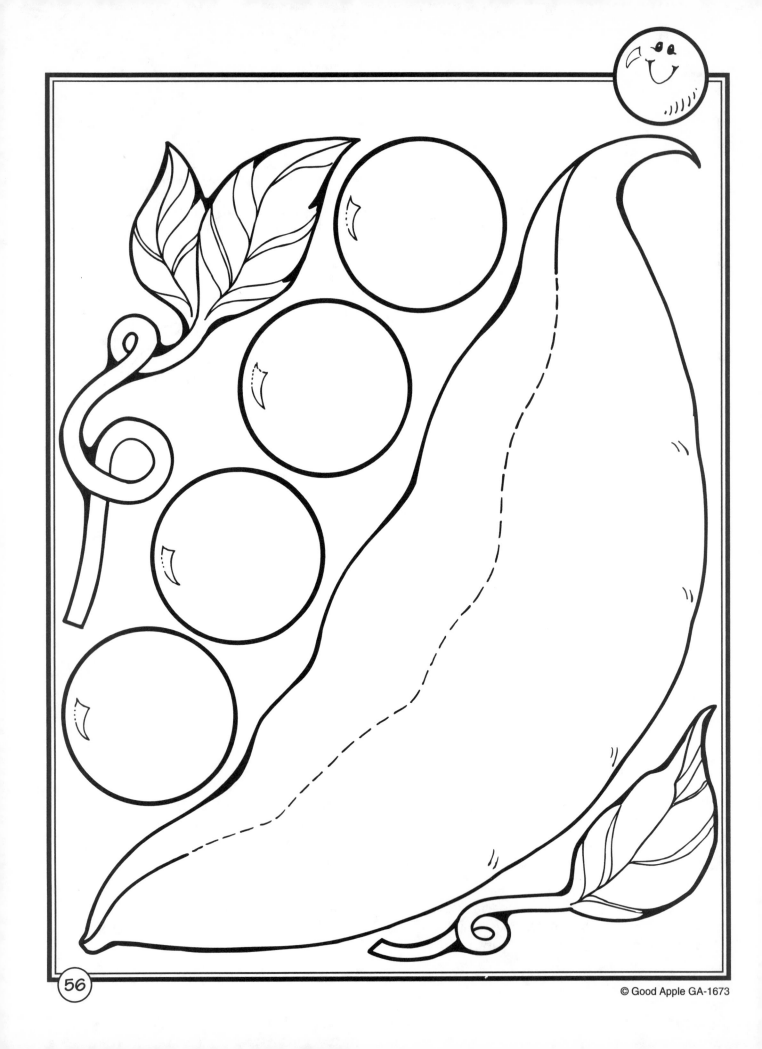

Problem of the Day

Q: Sal and Hal are two members of the Pal family. Sal is 8 years old, and Hal is 9 years old. What will Hal's age be when the total of the digits in both their ages is once again 17?

A: *Hal will be 18, and Sal will be 17.*

Q: Pick any number. Multiply it by 3. Add 7. Add the number you started with. Add 5. Divide by 4. Subtract the number you started with. What do you get?

A: *3*

Q: Find the patterns for the following:

　　a) 1, 4, 2, 5, 3, 6, 4, ____, ____

　　b) 100, 52, 28, 16, ____, ____

　　c) 5, 8, 6, 9, ____, ____

　　d) Z, 1, W, 3, T, 5, ____, ____

　　e) 0.5, 0.8, 0.6, 0.9, 0.7, ____, ____

A: *a) 7, 6 b) 10, 7 c) 7, 10 d) Q, 7 e) 1.0, 0.8*

Q: Tell the answer and the operation(s) for each.

　　a) There are 24 hours in a day and 365 days in a year. How many hours are in a year?

　　b) There are 99 players. There are 11 players on a team. How many teams are there?

　　c) Girl Scout cookies are $3.00 a box. You spend $36.00. How many boxes do you buy?

　　d) Candy hearts cost $.80 a bag. You buy 10 bags. How much do you spend?

　　e) You buy 12 dozen doughnuts. How many do you have?

　　f) There are 21 donkeys, 78 cows, and 90 porcupines. How many animals are there?

　　g) You have 45 bags of chocolate. Your little sister eats $\frac{1}{3}$ of the bags. How many do you have left?

A: *a) 8,760—multiply; b) 9—divide; c) 12—divide; d) $8.00—multiply; e) 144—multiply; f) 89—add; g) 30—divide and subtract*

Q: Mary made quilts and pillows. She was paid $50.00 for each quilt she made and $30.00 for each pillow. Mary has $410.00. How many quilts and how many pillows did she make?

A: *7 pillows and 4 quilts*

Problem of the Day

Q: Bob Gold charges $35.00 for a haircut. He charges an extra $5.00 for a blow dry. How much does he make if he has 12 customers who get a haircut and blow dry?

A: $480.00

Q: Warren cooks dinner for 45 people. He spends $100.00 on ingredients and charges each person $5.00 for the meal. How much profit does Warren make?

A: $125.00

Q: Bruce charges $150.00 to photograph a wedding. He shoots 11 weddings in the month of June. How much does Bruce make?

A: $1650.00

Q: Norma and her friend Susan play number games to have fun. They played the age game. Susan said that in three years, she would be twice Norma's age. How old are Norma and Susan now if in three years, their combined ages will be 24?

A: Susan is 13; Norma is 5.

Q: Sarah sold doughnuts. She wanted to make a pyramid of doughnuts with one at the very top and an additional one in each row. How many of her 36 doughnuts should be put on the bottom row?

A: 8

Q: Using a 3 x 3 square, arrange the odd numbers (1–17) so that they total 27 in all directions.

A:

7	17	3
5	9	13
15	1	11

Q: Tiny Tina ate 100 candy bars in five days. Each day, she ate six more than on the previous day. How many did she eat on each of the five days?

A: 8, 14, 20, 26, 32

Q: Kathy loves the number eight. How many 8s will she write if she writes the number 1 through 100?

A: 20

READ THE WORLD

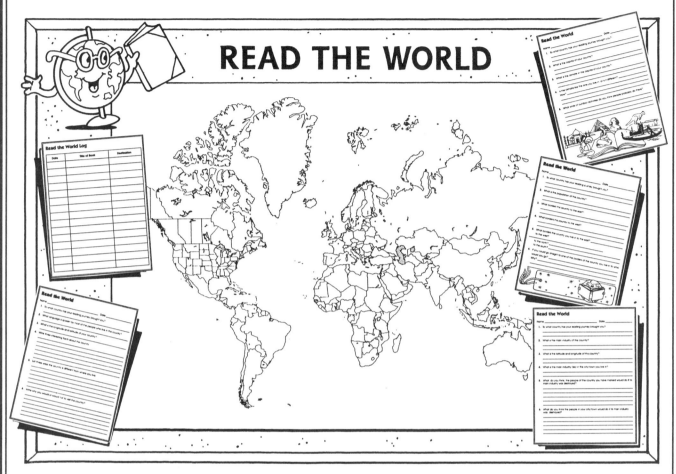

PURPOSE: To integrate geographical information with a reading incentive program

MATERIALS: large map of the world, one copy of the individual map of the world (page 61) per student, map pins, colored string, labels, one copy of page 60 per student; optional: copies of the activities on pages 62–66

DIRECTIONS: Have each student choose a country on which to begin his or her reading journey. Students can mark their spots with colored pins. Then tell students that they are required to read one novel, independently, per month. Each time a student finishes a book, he or she places a new pin on an adjacent country and connects his or her pins using colored string. Students will simply be trying to travel across the world, going from one country to an adjacent one each time they finish a book. Also, you may wish to prepare a *book information form* students must complete for each book they read. You could ask for such information as *title, author, main characters, setting, plot,* etc. Other ideas for book activities can be found on page 62. Students can record their progress on page 60. On their personal world maps, students can chart or color countries visited. Each month, incorporate a geography activity relating to their countries. Sample activities and activity pages can be found on pages 62–66.

Read the World Log

Date	Title of Book	Destination

Read the World Map

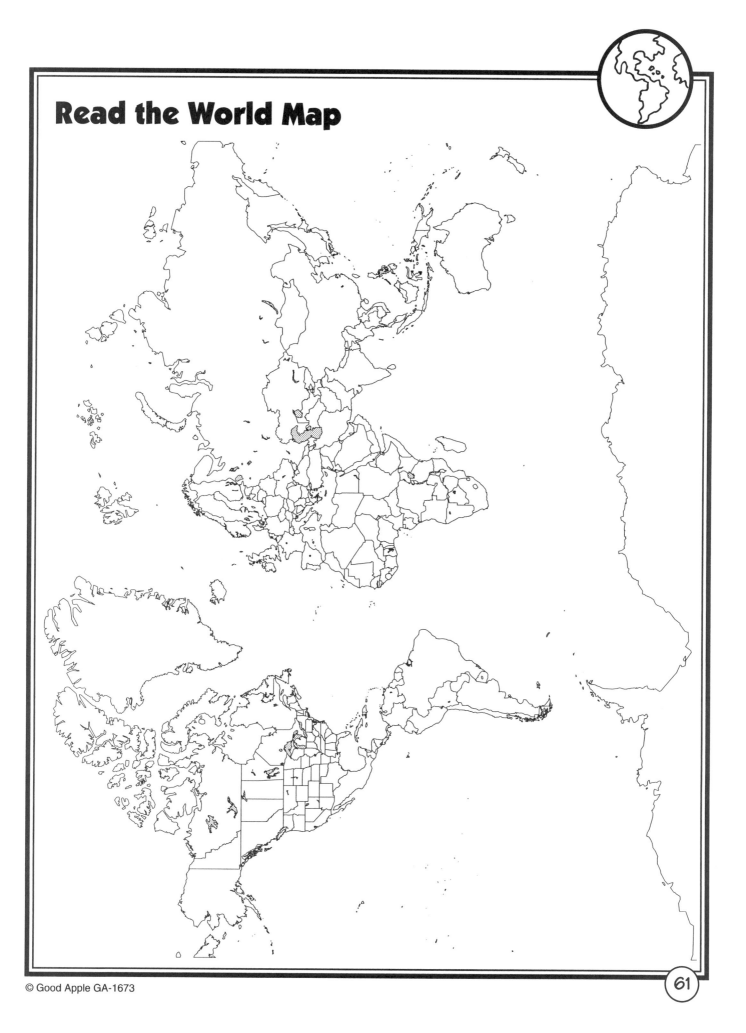

Book Report Ideas for Read the World

Title-Talk: Discuss why the author chose the title of the book you read. Give examples from the book. Also, tell whether you liked the title or not. Write a new title if you wish and explain why you selected this title.

Oral Report: Give an oral report to the class discussing your thoughts on the book. Be sure your report is three to five minutes in length.

Hanging Overhead: Make a mobile showing important scenes and characters from your book. Include 5–7 pictures.

Boxing: Make a diorama showing an important scene or event from your novel.

Book Commercial: Choose a book and advertise it in front of the class. You may wish to read a picture book or a chapter of a longer novel to entice your readers.

A Lasting Impression: Draw 3–5 illustrations depicting some important events in the book. Write a paragraph describing each illustration.

Sound Off: Discuss something you did not like about the book.

Everyone should read "Inside the Pyramid." It is exciting, fun, and . . .

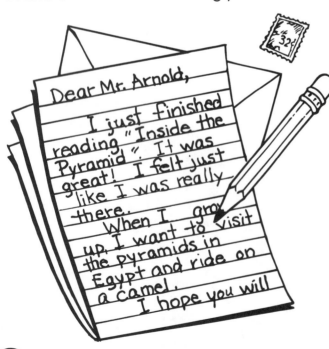

Dear Mr. Arnold,
I just finished reading "Inside the Pyramid." It was great! I felt just like I was really there. When I grow up, I want to visit the pyramids in Egypt and ride on a camel. I hope you will

Character Sketch: Write as if you are one of the characters; react to what happened to you in the book.

Dear Author: Write the author a letter about your feelings concerning the book.

Compare and Contrast: Choose two books of the same genre or that have been written by the same author. Compare and contrast them.

Lights, Camera, Action: Read the same book as a friend and "act out" a scene, complete with costume and setting.

Read the World

Name _____ Date _____

1. To what country has your reading journey brought you?
   _____

2. What language is spoken by most of the people who live in this country?
   _____

3. What is the longitude and latitude of your country?
   _____

4. Write three interesting facts about this country.
   _____
   _____
   _____
   _____
   _____
   _____

5. List three ways the country is different from where you live.
   _____
   _____
   _____
   _____
   _____
   _____

6. Write why you would or would not want to visit this country.
   _____
   _____
   _____
   _____
   _____
   _____

Read the World

Name _____ Date _____

1. To what country has your reading journey brought you?

    _____

2. What is the capital of your country?

    _____

3. What is the climate in the capital of your country?

    _____

    _____

4. Is the climate like the one you live in, or is it different? _____

    How? _____

    _____

    _____

    _____

5. What kinds of outdoor activities do you think people probably do there?

    _____

    _____

    _____

    _____

    _____

64

Read the World

Name _____ Date _____

1. To what country has your reading journey brought you?
   _____

2. What is the population of this country?
   _____

3. What borders this country to the east?
   _____

4. What borders this country to the west?
   _____

5. What borders the country you live in to the east? _____
   to the west? _____
   to the north? _____
   to the south? _____

6. If you could go straight to one of the borders of the country you live in, to
   which would you go? _____
   Why? _____
   _____
   _____
   _____
   _____

Read the World

Name _____ Date _____

1. To what country has your reading journey brought you?
   _____

2. What is the main industry(ies) of this country?
   _____
   _____

3. What is the latitude and longitude of this country?
   _____

4. What is the main industry(ies) in the city/town you live in?
   _____
   _____

5. What, do you think, the people of the country would do if its main industry was destroyed?
   _____
   _____
   _____
   _____
   _____
   _____
   _____

6. What do you think the people in your city/town would do if its main industry was destroyed?
   _____
   _____
   _____
   _____
   _____
   _____

PURPOSE: To establish a link between what is learned in school and its application in the real world

MATERIALS: magazines, one copy of page 68 per student

DIRECTIONS: This may be a good bulletin board to plan for open house. Have students cut out a variety of faces from magazines and decorate the bulletin board with them. Send home the letter and bubble (page 68) to parents and let them fill out the forms expressing their feelings about what they learned in school and how it is applied to "real life."

NOTE: An alternative is to have students at the end of the school year fill in the bubbles for upcoming students. They can describe the year's events and highlights and give suggestions to help them have a successful school year.

Real Life

Dear Parent(s),

One of the questions students frequently ask in school is "How will I use this in real life?" Here's your opportunity to let them know what you learned in school and how it applies to daily life as you know it! Please use the bubble below to write about some event and/or teacher that changed your life and helped you become the successful person you are today. Have your child cut out the bubble and return it to school by _____.

Thank you!

_____

Skeletons in the Closet

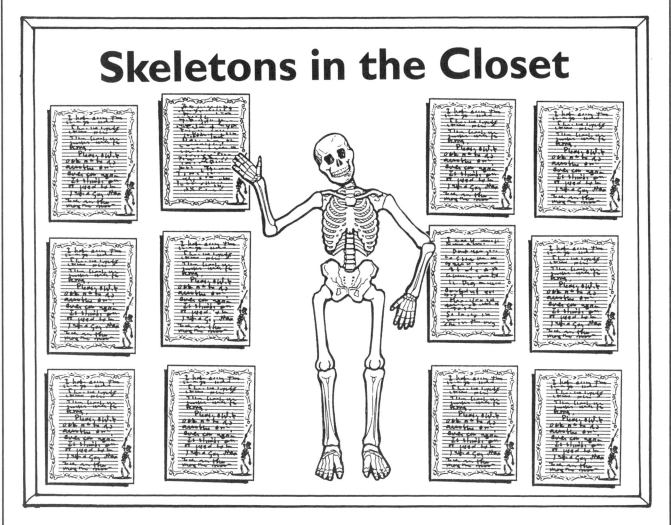

PURPOSE: To have students write Halloween stories from selected story starters

MATERIALS: copies of the story starters on pages 72–73, copies of the bone patterns on page 71, copies of the skeleton on page 74 to use as art on the bulletin board, copies of the stationery on page 70 for students, dark paper (to use to cover the bulletin board)

DIRECTIONS: Cut out as many bones as you need for the story starters you will use. Cut out each story starter (or create your own) and glue it onto a bone. Hang the bones story-starter-side down for mystery. Let each student select a bone/story starter to write a story about. Students can write their final drafts on the skeleton stationery. Remove the story starters from the bulletin board and replace them with students' stories.

NOTE: Play scary music while students make their skeletal selections. Also, students can make the skeleton the day before this activity. Hang it up with the story starters and stories.

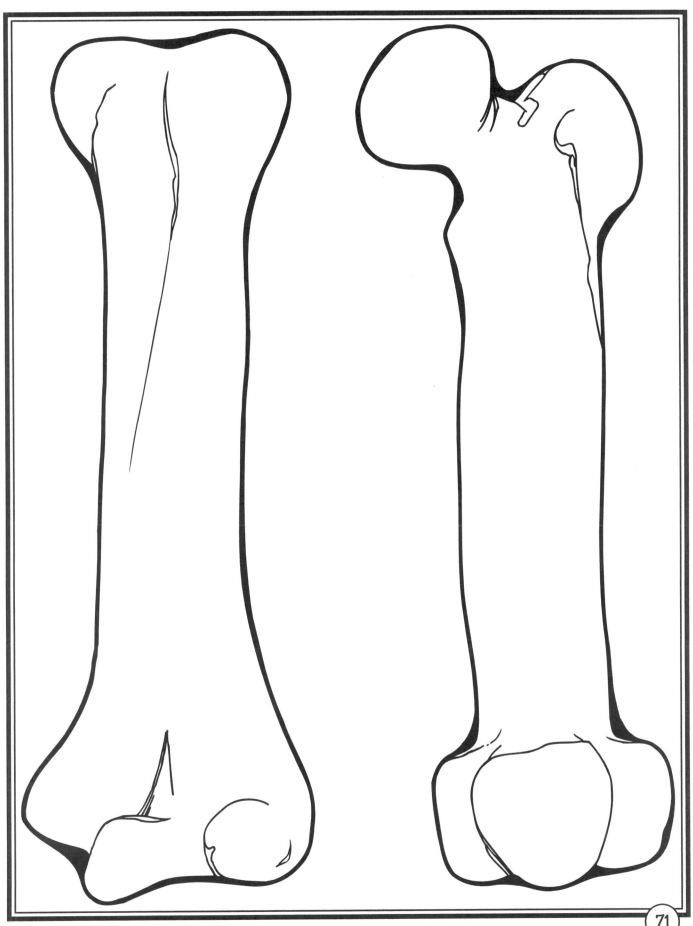

Skeletal Story Starters

I was the only one home when I heard the back door slam shut.

I awoke from a deep sleep to find something cool and sticky dripping onto my face from the ceiling.

I was filled with dread when the old woman's fingers dug into my arm.

The headlights of the car caught the strange and terrible creature running down the road with my sister in his arms.

We had walked into the woods that evening when we came across a mysterious green-black lake, almost hidden behind the dense mist.

This man seemed to be our father. He looked like him, talked like him, he even smelled like him, but I knew it wasn't my dad.

Somehow during the night, my nails had become long and clawlike, my teeth had become sharp fangs, and I had a strong craving for . . .

The bird came out of the tree, swooped down, and without warning, began to . . .

I heard something calling to me from the crumbling, moss-covered shack behind Grandfather's barn.

Skeletal Story Starters

I hadn't been back to the lake in years. I just hadn't had the courage since the time . . .

I screamed as I saw the enormous mummy step out of its tomb.

As I switched on my flashlight, the wide beam struck an old man approaching our tree house.

The horrible howling coming from my backyard sounded like my music teacher.

When I opened my brother's bedroom door, I saw that he had become no more than two inches tall.

Looking into the bedroom mirror, I noticed four green spots across my forehead.

My bicycle screeched to a halt as I noticed a shadowy figure in the upstairs window of the abandoned house.

Across the street, I saw a small, humanlike figure pace back and forth across the windowsill.

As I opened the can of spaghetti, I noticed that the contents were moving around noisily.

A dark figure appeared at my window, beckoning me to follow.

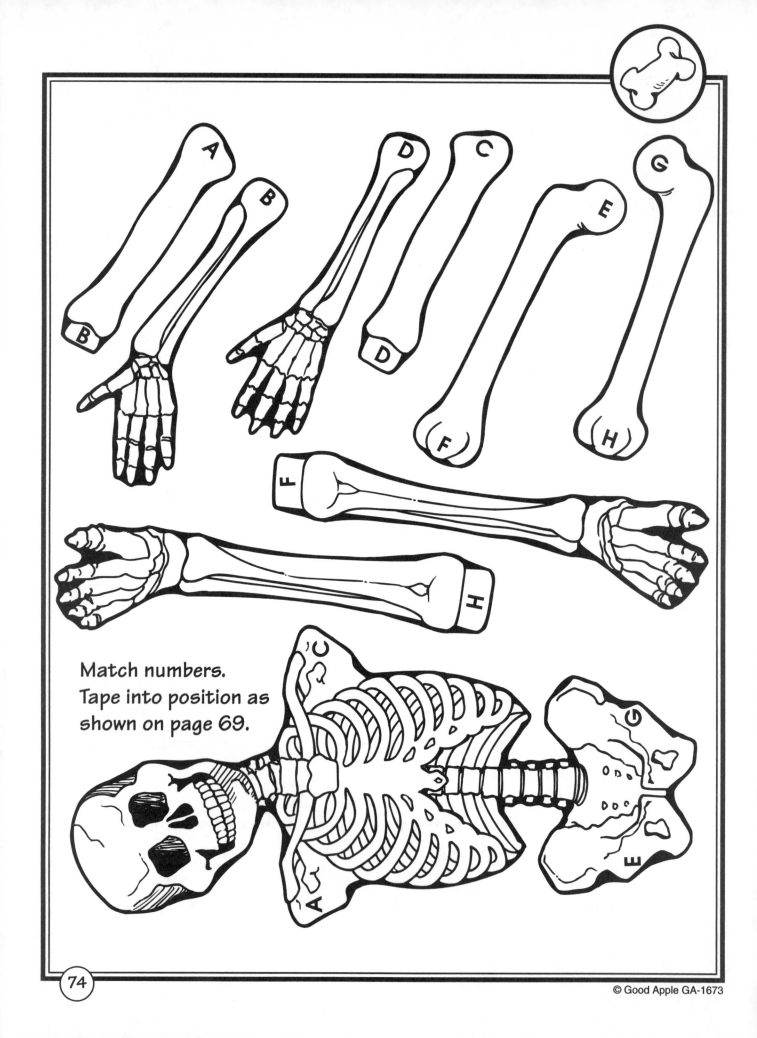

Match numbers.
Tape into position as
shown on page 69.

SPOTLIGHT ON . . .

PURPOSE: To get to know students individually and to help students become acquainted with one another

MATERIALS: one copy of page 76 per student, any items students choose to share (photos, book jackets, CD covers, ribbons, awards, etc.)

DIRECTIONS: Select a student each week to spotlight. Choosing the student on a Friday will allow him or her the opportunity to gather important personal items to share with the class. Hang the student's artifacts and completed spotlight sheet on the bulletin board on Monday. Have the class congregate around the board while the "Spotlight" student shares his or her personal items.

NOTE: Alternative titles: "Now Starring . . .", "Super Star," Up Close and Personal"

Spotlight on . . .

_____
name

My birthday is _____.

In my family, there are _____ people. I have _____ brothers and _____ sisters.

Three words to describe me are _____, _____, and _____.

A color that best describes me is _____.

I am most thankful for _____.

My favorite food is _____.

My favorite hobby is _____.

My most prized possession is _____.

My favorite movie is _____.

If I could star in any movie, I'd be _____.

If I had one wish, it would be _____.

If I could go on vacation anywhere, I would choose _____

_____.

My favorite memory is _____.

_____

_____.

VOCAB-U-DRAGON

PURPOSE: To enhance vocabulary development (This board is perfect to do in conjunction with a novel study, spelling words, or weekly vocabulary words.)

MATERIALS: large sheets of butcher paper, an assortment of colored construction paper, scale and dragon patterns (pages 78–79)

DIRECTIONS: Copy the dragon pattern on a transparency. Then enlarge the dragon to the size of the bulletin board to be used and cut it out. Provide students with different colored scraps/squares of construction paper as well as a circle tracer they can use to create the scales. Assign students vocabulary words as well as the definitions to be copied on the scales. (See page 79 for an example of where to write the words and definitions on the scales.) Fold scales in half and staple them onto the dragon's body.

NOTE: This looks terrific with a black background and brightly colored paper for the body and scales. Metallic paper can be also purchased. This bulletin board is great to use when doing a novel study of *In the Year of the Boar and Jackie Robinson, The Paper Bag Princess,* or fairy tale/fantasy studies.

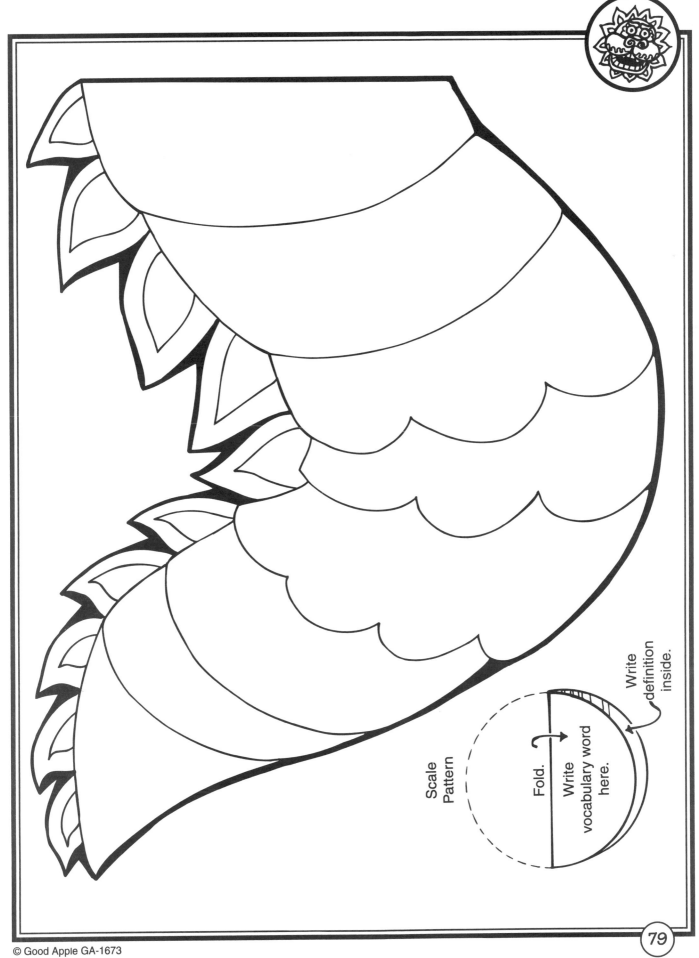

Scale
Pattern

Fold.

Write
vocabulary word
here.

Write
definition
inside.

WHAT'S OUR MOTTO? WIN THE LOTTO!

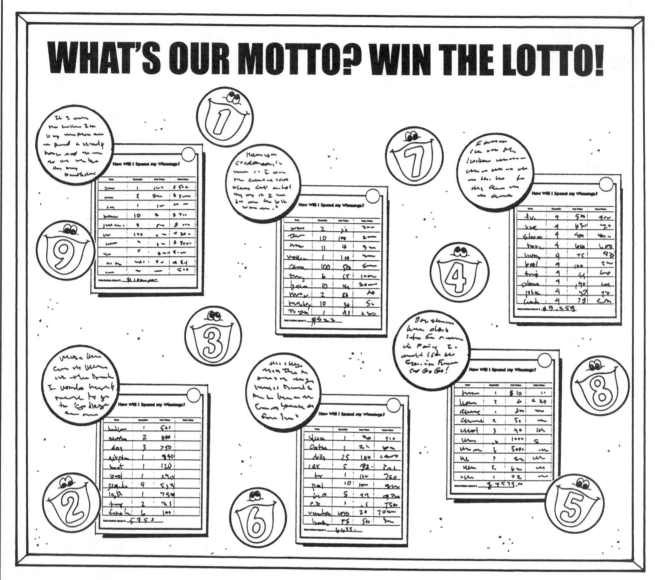

PURPOSE: To have students think creatively about what they would do if they won the lottery

MATERIALS: one copy of page 81 per student, one copy of the lotto ball pattern on page 82 per student

DIRECTIONS: This bulletin board is perfect to use as a creative writing/math activity. Discuss with students what they would do if they won the lottery (give a specified amount). Allow students time to research and itemize how they would spend their winnings. Students can record this on page 81. Students can then write stories on their lotto balls (page 82) telling how they would spend their winnings. Hang students' final drafts, along with their budget sheets, on the bulletin board.

How Will I Spend My Winnings?

Name _____

Item	Quantity	Unit Price	Total Price

Total Dollars Spent $ _____

WHAT'S THE SCOOP?

PURPOSE: To have students share their opinions about current movies, books, fads, computer games, personal achievements, etc.

MATERIALS: one copy of the patterns on pages 84–85 per student (use a variety of colors), red construction paper

DIRECTIONS: Brainstorm with students a list of current events, movies, books, computer games, etc. Explain to students that this is their opportunity to share their opinions about current happenings. Each day, or every few days, feature one of the events on the list. Students' opinions can all be shared on their "ice cream scoops." Students can also respond to their classmate's reviews by writing their opinions on "cherries" they make out of red construction paper.

NOTE: An alternative would be to have students use scoops for book reports.

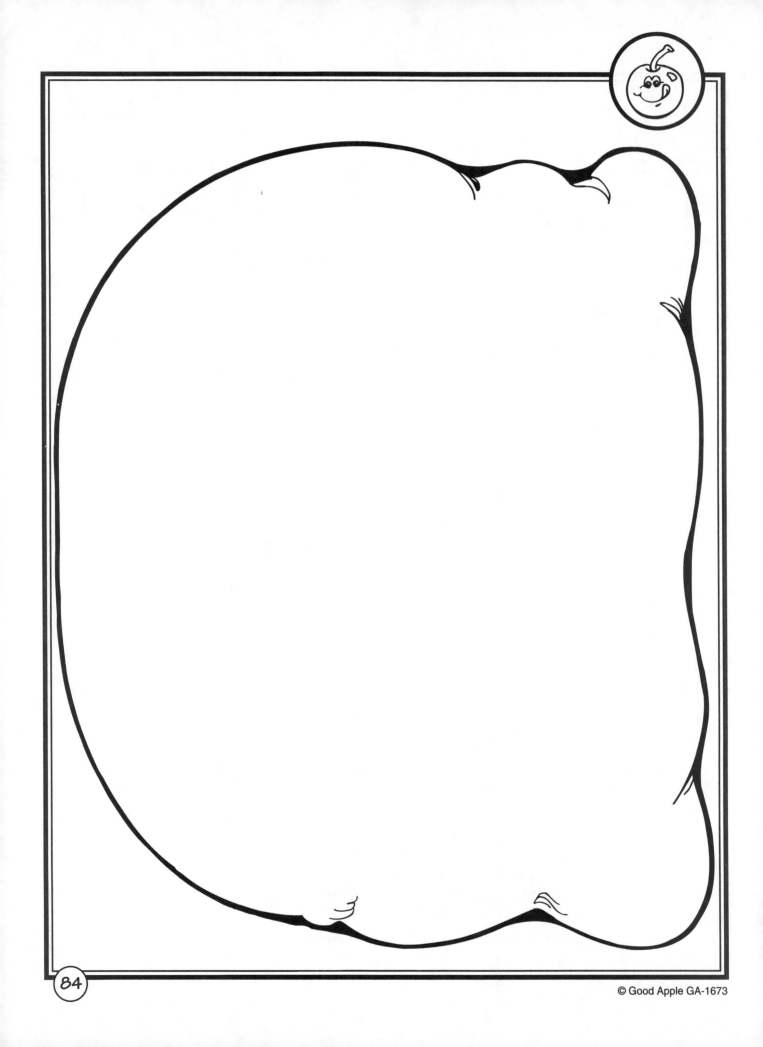

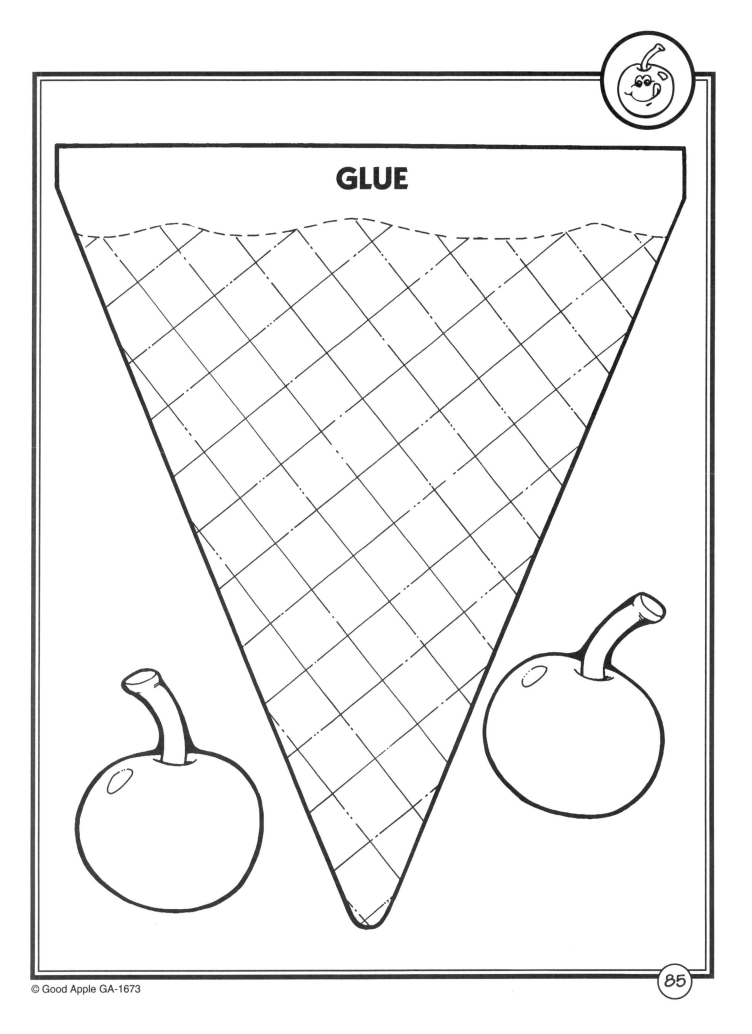

GLUE

HEART SMART

9. Your heart is about the size of your
a. brain
b. fist
c. foot

PURPOSE: To have students use a variety of resources to answer questions about the heart and related topics

MATERIALS: 28 or so copies of the heart pattern on page 90, one copy of the list of heart-related questions on pages 87–89, Optional: one copy of the "Heart Smart" cover on page 90 for each student

DIRECTIONS: Prior to explaining this activity to students, make enough copies of the heart pattern so that you can write each question from pages 87–89 on a numbered heart and hang it on the bulletin board. Then explain to students that for each day of the month of February (or any month of your choice), they will select a "Heart Smart" question posted on the bulletin board. Students should write their answers either in notebooks or in student-made booklets. (You can use the "Heart Smart" cover on page 90 if students will be making their own booklets.) Designate the number of questions that you expect students to complete for this activity. For example, perhaps you want students to complete 15 of the 28 questions by a particular date. Students' collected work can then be displayed.

NOTE: Students may work with partners or individually. Have students complete this activity during available free time. Hearts may be hung on string and numbered, allowing students to flip over the heart for the question they select. Questions do not necessarily have to be answered in numerical order which will allow individual students to work on different questions each day.

Heart Smart Questions

1. Your heart is about the size of your a. brain. b. fist. c. foot.

   answer: b. fist

2. What are the four chambers of the human heart?

   answer: right atrium, left atrium, right ventricle, left ventricle

3. Count how many times your heart beats in thirty seconds. Using this information, how many times does it beat in five minutes, thirty minutes, and one hour?

   Answers will vary.

4. Why do you put your hand on your heart when you say the "Pledge of Allegiance"?

   answer: out of respect for our country

5. Think of four expressions that include the word "heart."

   possible answers: half-hearted, heartily

6. Write an acrostic poem for the word "heart." Be sure the poem makes sense!

   Answers will vary.

7. Write 10 words using the letters in the phrase "Heart Smart."

   possible answers: ear, treat, hear, rare, etc.

8. Name a song with the word "heart" in the title.

   Answers will vary.

9. Name a movie with the word "heart" in the title.

   Answers will vary.

Heart Smart Questions

10. **Name a book with the word "heart" in the title.**

    Answers will vary.

11. **Describe your favorite "hearty" meal.**

    Answers will vary.

12. **How much do you think your heart weighs?**
    a. less than one pound, b. more than one pound, c. five pounds

    answer: a. less than one pound

13. **What do you think a heart symbolizes?**

    Answers will vary.

14. **Make a heart that is no taller than eight inches and no wider than five inches. Be creative and colorful!**

    Hearts will vary.

15. **What is the name given to a doctor who specializes in heart disease?**

    answer: cardiologist

16. **What does the term "cardiovascular diseases" have to do with your heart?**

    answer: Cardiovascular diseases refer to one who has heart disease.

17. **Name five other organs besides the heart.**

    possible answers: liver, kidney, intestine, stomach, pancreas, etc.

18. **In what city did Frank Sinatra leave his heart?**

    answer: San Francisco

Heart Smart Questions

19. In a deck of cards, how many cards are hearts?

    answer: 13

20. What are hearts of palm?

    answer: a type of vegetable

21. What is the definition of "heartland?"

    answer: a central or vital area

22. Look up the word "heart" and write a complete definition for it.

    Answers will vary depending on the dictionary used.

23. Write the name of a poem with the word "heart" in it. Include the title and author.

    Answers will vary.

24. What kinds of people run a greater risk of having a heart attack? a. those who are overweight, b. those who are too thin, c. those who exercise continuously

    answer: a. those who are overweight

25. True/False: A heart shape is symmetrical. If true, draw a heart and its line of symmetry.

    answer: true

26. True/False: A heart shape can tessellate.

    answer: false

27. Write the name of a city in the U.S. that has "heart" (or "hart") in it.

    Answers will vary.

28. What type of exercise is good for your heart?

    answer: aerobic

Heart
Pattern

Heart
Smart
by

name

BABY FACE

PURPOSE: To get to know students individually and to help students become acquainted with one another at the beginning of the school year

MATERIALS: photograph of each child as an infant or toddler, copies of the "Baby Talk" forms on pages 94–96, one copy of the parent letter on page 92 per student, one copy of page 93 per student

DIRECTIONS: Send home the letter to parents along with one of the "Baby Talk" forms asking parents to assist with this project. Explain to students that they should not show other students their pictures or their "Baby Talk" forms. Hang students' pictures and their "Baby Talk" forms on the board. Write a number next to each student. Allow time for students to read each one, look at each picture, and guess who's who on the "Guess Who!" sheet (page 93). Go through each number, asking a few students to share their guesses. After sharing guesses, have the real "baby" stand up.

NOTE: You may choose to turn this into a contest for "Cutest Baby," "Biggest Eyes," etc. In addition, you may have students bring in a favorite toy or blanket from when they were little to put on display. Have students write short stories from a baby's point of view. Hang these next to the pictures.

Dear Parents,

We are looking forward to getting to know our classmates better by sharing some of our earliest experiences and memories with them. In doing so, could you please send in a picture of your child as an infant or a toddler? Also, your child will need your assistance in filling out the attached form entitled, "Baby Talk." Pictures will be displayed for a short period of time and will be returned. Pictures must be appropriate for classroom display.

The identities of the photos will be kept secret, as part of the project will be for the children to guess who the pictures are of. Please send your child's photo in a sealed envelope with your child's name written on the outside.

Thank you!

_____
(Name)

Guess Who!

Name _____

Look carefully at each picture on the board. Guess which classmate matches each picture.

Baby 1:

_____

Baby 2:

_____

Baby 3:

_____

Baby 4:

_____

Baby 5:

_____

Baby 6:

_____

Baby 7:

_____

Baby 8:

_____

Baby 9:

_____

Baby 10:

Baby 11:

_____

Baby 12:

_____

Baby 13:

_____

Baby 14:

_____

Baby 15:

_____

Baby 16:

_____

Baby 17:

_____

Baby 18:

_____

Baby 19:

_____

Baby 20:

Baby 21:

_____

Baby 22:

_____

Baby 23:

_____

Baby 24:

_____

Baby 25:

_____

Baby 26:

_____

Baby 27:

_____

Baby 28:

_____

Baby 29:

_____

Baby 30:

Baby Talk

When I was a baby, I...	often	sometimes	never
CRIED			
SLEPT			
LAUGHED			
SMILED			

94

Baby Talk

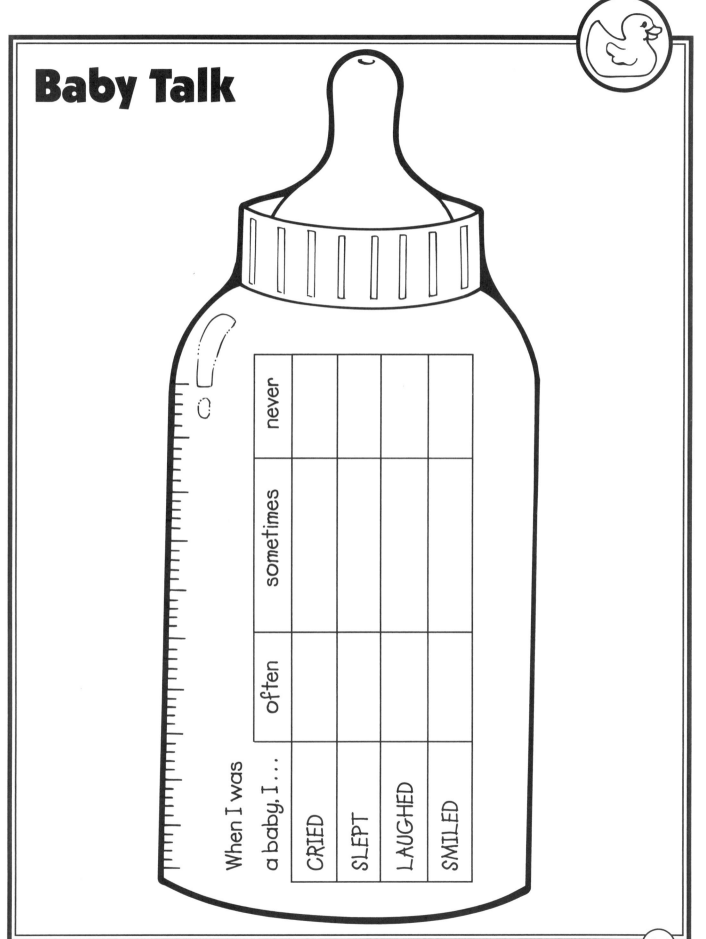

When I was a baby, I . . .	often	sometimes	never
CRIED			
SLEPT			
LAUGHED			
SMILED			

Baby Talk

When I was a baby, I . . .

a baby, I . . .	often	sometimes	never
CRIED			
SLEPT			
LAUGHED			
SMILED			